Calling into the Dark

Calling into the Dark

POEMS BY

Martha Orton

Last Leaf PRESS

• Chestertown, MD •

Last Leaf
P R E S S

Printed in the United States of America.

FIRST PAPERBACK EDITION

Series Editor: Jeff Coomer
Layout and Design Editor: Sarah Crossland

Library of Congress Control Number: 2018934517
Last Leaf Press, Chestertown, MD

ISBN 978-0-9965708-1-7

Please note that these writings are expressions of subjective experiences formulated from the author's thoughts and imaginings and are not intended to portray real individuals or events or to be accurate representations. The names used are fictional and are included for their rhythmic or other poetic qualities.

I would like to thank Last Leaf Press for their support in publishing my poetry, particularly Jeff Coomer, for his thoughtful review of the collection and advice in the selection of poems, and Sarah Crossland for her excellent design. The literary knowledge and design skill of both are greatly appreciated. I also express my sincere appreciation for everyone who has enriched my experience of life and helped me to develop some understanding of this extraordinarily complex world, especially my husband Robert and all my sons.

To my Mother
in
gratitude
for her courageous and loving heart
and
her love
of all things blue
including bluegrass music

Contents

For who could live or breathe if there were not this delight of existence as the ether in which we dwell?

From Delight all these beings are born, by Delight they exist and grow, to Delight they return.

Taittiriya Upanishad
Translated by Sri Aurobindo

I

Mental Health

Another day, another fifty cents—
one of my fellow therapists
used to say back when we
both were underpaid toilers
in an underfunded system,
given a pittance to save
the citizenry from suicide,
hazards of mania, depression,
anxiety and the consequences
of all varieties of abuse,
as well as other ills and torments.
Then after a day in the trenches
we would drift out the door,
fumble for the car keys,
make our way home and
try to save ourselves.

Fuzzy

The therapists I knew
used to all be
fuzzy-haired and middle-aged.
Now somehow that's changed.
The look has become more glam,
even fashion-conscious,
as the new ones join the ranks.
Gone are the crumpled cardigans,
the humorous colorful socks.
Now they look more in control,
better groomed and successful.
Are they trying to convince us,
the old guard, that they
really know the score,
really get the human psyche
even better now that
the New Age is old?

Changes

The barista who greeted me with *namaste*
is gone from the unaccountably unpopular cafe.
So are the scones and crescent buns,
the useless handmade mug holders,
the pile of random unread books.
The new owners have a strange view
of what this pleasant place should be.
Now wine bottles are gathering
behind the tall wooden counter,
lining up in solemn rows
with artisan beers in front.
Sometimes you just want everything
to stay dependably the same.
Missing the barista, I totter out
into the sunshine empty-handed.

Ogunquit Summer

Flame-haired dreamer riding through the night,
motorbike skirting the grilled steel that
fills the span of the arcing bridge
from Maine to New Hampshire.

So young, so long ago the roller-skating
messenger in the halls of the mental ward
where you may or may not have stayed for months
for a cure for your depression or worse.

Problems only obliquely mentioned were
somehow in the background as we nearly
ran off the road at four in the morning,
you fully asleep, nodding and dreaming.

Good Friends

Four good friends,
four glasses of Cabernet Sauvignon,
four plates of fresh ravioli,
two dozen asparagus spears,
two hundred and sixty years
of vivid, meaningful experiences
to share over the broad dinner table—
successes, apparent failures,
wishes, hopes for our children and
of course also for ourselves, all
bundled intertwining in amiable
to and fro while building friendship,
a sense of purpose,
a structure of meaning.

His Struggle

Teasing out more from the day,
tempting fate by staying up late,
I read endless tales of Norway
told tediously in translation.
Youthful trials and misadventures
unfold in intimate detail,
leaving me unenvious
and not sorry to have grown up
in a small Appalachian town
where children also suffered
similar indignities,
though with a good deal less snow.
In a way it's comforting to see
that some growing pains are universal.
So for now I weep for Karl Ove,
but not for me.

The Room

The floral diamonds on the patterned carpet gleam
softly in the summer sunlight sifting
through the cobwebbed window
where the ever-enlarging spider
consumes caterpillars.

The worn brown knobs on the ladder-back
chair from my childhood glow as muted crowns
above the forever-fraying rush seat
still holding firm where
I wait for you.

Ending its circling the fly
alights on the dog dreamlessly drowsing
on the ombre-striped sofa
in the early morning stillness while
I wait for you.

Fiftieth Class Reunion

Gray heads with twinkling eyes,
wry and knowing smiles—
we all knew each other
way back when, young and foolish,
we tackled academe as if
it was ours to master,
to relish each and every
pain and delight in the process
of coming together in ancient halls,
of embracing furtively or openly
under towering trees, our shelter
from pelting coastal rains,
from scorching summer sun.
Now we gather again
loving each other differently,
more wisely and for better reasons.
Oh, if I had known then
so much of what I know now,
I would have loved you all
for who you are,
and also myself.

Good Dad

Standing on a snow pile,
clutching a stack of seven frozen pizzas,
freezing in shrink-wrapped finery
tightly held in his arms,
he says, "We've all got cabin fever.
Now we're having company.
So I got these."
Looking wide-eyed and baffled,
brown eyes below Nordic cap,
dark overcoat draping around him,
he looks amused at himself,
bemused by the pizza stack,
unable to explain fully
just why.

Towers

Draper's Mountain loomed in the distance
every morning of my childhood,
its fire tower unseen far away.
We climbed it once fearfully,
braving its wind-battered ladders
high above the valley and the town.
My cousin Billy manned his tower
in the Forest Service in Kentucky.
Alone he consumed a summer's rations
in a mere four weeks.
Was he really so hungry,
or perhaps bored and lonely?
It's now too late to ask.

Brother

Sitting by the edge of the road
his lunch box by his side,
the little boy had taken his stand,
voted with his feet and left home.
He had turned his back on complaint,
on criticism for being left-handed,
on being upbraided for most anything
to do with being a small boy and imperfect.
Maybe one of the neighbors
down the street could use a new son,
someone to bring a laugh or a smile
into a dull or lonely day.
Maybe there was someone
who could love him as much
as he deserved to be loved,
someone who knew that small boys,
as well as small girls, are naturally
works in progress.

Belle

Grandmother always said:
You have to take your good time with you,
speaking to me as a dour adolescent
timidly facing yet another party.
I seem to have inherently misunderstood,
for all I am able to do is
take my misery with me,
the good times having somehow
fallen by the wayside.
This would disappoint her sorely
were she alive today,
for she was easily
the belle of the ball.

Gentleman

The flannel-shirted chap was six feet with sandy hair,
delft blue eyes, enlivened by a wry sense of humor.
He took a benevolent, yet cautious, view of life.
His lady wife was barely five feet in her shoes,
but she was a firebrand
and usually got her way.
An implication here, an offhand criticism there,
a tinge of disapproval or passionate endorsement
eddy and swirl in the flow
of outer thought and depths of mind,
building or unbuilding a case, maneuvering position
to lead to a wanted conclusion, a desired aim.
Kind and gentle men need be wary, to look out
for the wiles of the charming, apparently demure,
the supposedly less powerful.
They have means at their disposal
unknown to the principled and true
natural gentlemen of this world.
Quietly laying the groundwork,
small piece by even smaller,
for preferences and desires,
they can play a long game
to win in the end.

Want Not

He was a fine looking boy, my father.
Thin and straight as a sapling,
he stands there in the photo
perpetually on his way to school,
bare feet grounding him to earth,
a cloth cap shielding his bright eyes
and in one hand a flour sack
holding two thick and fragrant
biscuits spread with apple butter
by his mother's deft hands
every morning, every day.
The same skilled hands sliced
his father's tired, worn trousers,
hemming them to be a boy's
in a waste-not, want-not world.

Relative

She was not a family favorite,
far from it, if truth be told,
but one of them after all.
They reflected on this especially
attending her funeral
under a spare green canopy
out in the misting April rain.
She must have had strengths and virtues
that they did not see
from their side of the divide,
a virtual chasm of distance
dug by years of looking askance
at reputed venality,
rumors of shameless self-promotion.
Yet she was treasured by her dearest.
So what do we, can we, know
about anyone around us?
How can we possibly assess,
possibly judge each other,
since we cannot know the truth?

Shiny Bright

The cardboard box lid says *Shiny Bright,*
New Bergen, New Jersey, and boasts the words
Made in America under a drawing of
Uncle Sam and Santa Claus shaking hands.
Looking elegant, Uncle Sam bends solicitously
from the waist while Santa Claus is his usual self.
Inside are the six remaining clear glass
ornaments, made during World War II and
consequently sporting little paper caps from
which they hang by string, instead of any form
of more durable metal attachment.
Yet endure they have, and I love them in all
their simple and spare hopefulness for a
happy Christmas in wartime.
One has a faint dusting of fake snow
which once glittered in contrast to blue glass
now faded to gray, though the memory
gleams on.

Subterranea

Eighty-four miles of books
tightly assembled underground,
row upon row of shelving
holding compressed knowledge
deep under Bryant Park,
stand there at attention
awaiting the call to service,
while you and I blithely
feast on sandwiches and tea
comfortably in the shade
of stately sycamores,
unaware of the vigilant
treasures beneath our feet.

Small Things

Tendrils of tediousness
twist tightly around thoughts
tirelessly traveling towards
a neverland of mental misery.
Wondrously winding wherever
they can, gripping and grasping
as they squeeze out the energy
enervating everything
hopeful and fine.
Petulant puddles of pettiness
form beneath the suffocated
boughs so fully entangled,
posing obstacles for the
pensive petitioner of
the future, who then must be
caught up in detour, delays,
dallying on the way and
losing track of the direction.
Big dreams are fine,
but it's the small things
that trip you up and
make you fail.

Truly

If I were to say how I truly feel,
would it frighten you away, upset you,
or make you see me
in a different light?

If I were to say how I truly feel,
would it really be true or just
some fleeting impulse
from a worrisome ego?

If I were to say what I really think,
would you agree or not, I wonder,
or maybe just sit there
being quietly tolerant?

If I were to say what I really think,
maybe you would love it and be glad
to have such a forthright,
honest and brave companion.

Tentative

Carefully crafting a message for you,
tediously puzzling over nuance,
furrowing my brow over tense and tone,
I finally, fatefully click to send
my latest version of strained opinion.
Waiting wearily, worrying about a
response and how this will seem when it comes,
I salute what I imagine to be
your well-earned, much-deserved self-confidence,
superior to my tired self-doubt.
So I lift my glass and say,
So be it.

Mere Words

Do words really live on forever
in the memory or on the page?
Once regretted can they ever
be forgotten, undone, erased?

Some so shallow, painful, unmeant
grow in strength, power over time,
changing into newly potent forms
of misery, sadness and grief.

Regret is a bitter poison drink
and so is misunderstanding
and the feeling that one's thoughts
were completely misread.

Hearing Test

The pleasures of a hearing test—
sweet silence of a sound-proof chamber,
opportunity to absorb the appearance of
a box of hand sanitizer affixed
straight ahead on the opposite fabric wall,
chance to sit still with very little to do
apart from repeating two-syllable words,
listening to occasional beeps and pushing a button,
learning the correct pronunciation
of tinnitus.

Plus Ultra

Intertwining voices ring out
in Latinate intricacy
rising and falling as they
wind around each other
recreating chants from Spain
first offered up six hundred
years ago and continuing
to enchant with their beauty,
vibrancy and charm.
Ardent singers, tireless in
your dedication to your art,
unceasing in devotion
to its loftiness and challenge,
we thank you.

String Quartet

At Cabell Hall on a Tuesday night,
masses of gray heads sit silently
attending to the young quartet
as they expertly render Hayden,
DeBussy and Beethoven
with deft technical excellence.
As the last strains barely fall silent
the listeners rise with one accord,
offering their traditional
unflinching standing ovation.
The nubile artists bow and
withdraw as the house lights appear.
Then with unforeseen energy,
rising with amazing alacrity,
the audience transforms into
a geriatric stampede.

A Song of Gladness

We sing a madrigal, our voices lilting
in four-part harmony drifting across
the expanse of nursing home dining room,
encompassing the white-haired listeners
seated so stilly waiting for
the next song and then the next.
Some smile, some nod, some drowse
so quietly we wonder if they are
breathing, as we inhale deeply
and prepare to begin again.
Hoping for more of a response,
we launch into Gershwin and Berlin.
Emboldened by the resultant animation
and invigorated by the foot-tapping,
we confidently conclude with
Mozart.

At the Dairy Godmother

In an ice cream parlor in Alexandria
today I sit in a chair where once
President Obama sat.
I don't know what flavor he enjoyed
on that special day, but I delight
in consuming a coffee milkshake,
slowly sipping, savoring, reflecting
on his nobility and appreciation
of truly good ice cream.
It's nice to have something in common
with a President.

Sorbet

If a day which includes ice cream
can't be considered a bad day,
what is a day with sorbet?
If a mild disaster strikes can it
redeem the day in some fashion?
Does it have the capacity
to make you smile in spite of yourself,
to ease your sad and weary heart,
to calm your stressed and frazzled nerves
and help you settle yourself down into
a reverie of simple gratitude,
at least for this?
Well, not as much,
but I'll take some,
give it a shot,
try it and see.
If it helps you,
maybe it will help me.

Traveling

So I will drink wine and think of Copenhagen,
reflecting on scenes of colorful Nyhaven,
on the bright windows of Amalienborg Palace
glinting in the warm strength of summer sunshine,
then the evening charm of the lights of Tivoli
in contrast with Christiansborg's somberness,
relieved by the liveliness of Radhuspladsen,
the City Hall Square with its varied complexities
of activity, creativity and hubbub—
strollers, cyclists, musicians, single and joined,
a fine mix of humanity, flocking together
in this civilized place, where I have often gone
while deep in thought on my sofa of green velvet.

II

Quake

The friend's poetry
confirms our world view
and style of expression.
His language and experience
resonate with our own.
How pleasant it is to discuss
points of true convergence
over vegetable lasagna
and glasses of good wine.
But what is happening
in the world beyond us
is shaking the foundation
of the lives we were born into,
rearranging the pieces
continually on the game board
as we reassess again
and always again.

Commonly

The churning roar of the pot
ends with a click and a rumble
as steam billows swirl
on their way to a cup.
Muted morning sounds, rustles upstairs,
comfortable, familiar,
form a preamble of the day.
This is the easy part,
the getting started.
What comes next, obligatory
first, next, later,
or, more importantly, but deferred,
what do I choose to fill the day—
confront the sense of being, of meaning,
of who, why, and what is it all about?
Some say the answers lie in the simple process
of forward movement,
of one step after another
to see where it leads.
Walk to the table,
put down the cup
then lift it again,
breathe the steam,
taste the tea.

Couple

She held onto him for dear life
with a flaming passion of possession
when they were first lovers and all was new
for them with a magnificent wonder
that they had finally found each other.
He bought her an absolutely artsy ring,
the single diamond creatively ensconced
and gleaming with symbolic splendor
as they strolled wintry streets arm in arm.
The breakup came suddenly, resounding sharply
like a rock fracturing plate glass.
But things have settled down now
and it's all pretty quiet
with joint custody
and alternate weekends
of loneliness.

Precedents

What is this obsession with the past—
old books, old houses, old families.
All this old stuff can choke the present
in a totally suffocating way,
squeezing the very life
out of a fine new day,
strangling the future before
it can even take a breath.

What is this fascination with the past—
old treasures, old artifacts, old people.
All this old stuff can inform the present
in a completely enriching way,
offering cautionary tales, wisdom
to build a better life, a new day,
if only it doesn't hold us back
with its sheer mass and weight.

Pretensions

So what persona is here today,
one formed by the same old role from the past
held up as a shaky shield
against present reality?
Is it some fragile defense
crudely constructed over time
to conceal the real self?
Or today is it just me,
simply being and doing,
straight up, sincere?
I need to be this,
to ditch the baggage
of past iterations.
I need to do this,
to keep the faith.

Under the Sign

From the warmth of the glowing bistro
shedding its light onto the pavement
through the window I see him alone
on a bench under the street light
illumining him and the sign for
the antique trail, the Three Chopt Road.

Red hair, white face, round form,
bare knees in the coldness,
he sits waiting, for what—
for friends, for time to pass,
for he knows not what—perhaps
hoping for something new
to break the tedium,
to end the solitude,
to begin a new chapter,
or at least turn the page,
for this lonely waiting figure,
this expectant, heavily sad
young man in the cold.

Inside, glasses are lifted
by hands both slender and broad.
Inside, eyes sparkle and wink,

sharing fond intimacies,
friend to friend, lover to lover,
mother to child, husband to wife.
There is closeness, comfort, joining,
knowing, wanting, keeping near,
with bonds both loose and secure.

Outside there is stillness in the cold night,
loneliness for this young man, with pale face
red hair, round form, weighed down by solitude.

Again Regret

Fatigue fuels forgetfulness
but not forgetting,
leading to regret.
Once again self-doubt
intrudes upon joy,
needlessly dimming
the light of this day,
pointlessly bringing
a remorseless gloom.
Push hard against it,
this massive boulder
blocking the way.
Struggle and resist
the falsehood of despair
masquerading as truth,
as a comfortable
familiar sadness,
for it is really
all a lie.

Invasive

Despair wound itself around his mind
like honeysuckle around a tree.
Seeming sweet and offering rest
in the guise of surrendering
to vulnerability just for awhile,
it gradually became suffocating,
stifling new growth and sapping energy
needed for renewal and hopefulness.
It has taken over now,
covered the whole canopy
with its sinuous tendrils,
and only very rarely
lets in a beam of sunlight.

Criticism

Curtailing creativity,
quashing it with a cruel critique
may help save the world from
inundation by mediocre
works of the pen and brush,
while serving the dual purpose of
giving corrective jolts to egos.
But what about the poor creators
and their need for self-expression—
a genuine drive to push forward
with or without an audience.
So write and paint to your heart's content
and be content with that.

Pale Lamentation

Late night confessions
of weakness and past sins
cannot resolve the
internal struggle
for validation.

Solitarily shed
tears count for little
without actions to
make amends, right wrongs,
heal wounds or even
extinguish hot fires
of anger, discord.

Please do not burden
me with these useless
prostrations; go
instead and
slay a dragon.

Young Again

evening comes
dusk descends
with the lightning bugs
an old longing
to be young
fair-haired
among brothers and friends
calling into the dark
playing tag
falling on the grass
as the dew begins to form
fresh free in the greenness
all on one's own
secure in the frolic
the boundless joy
of running tumbling
without any plan

Holding On

How can you carry the past
with you into the future?
Can it be draped lightly over
the shoulders like a fine shawl
without becoming a crushing weight,
or need it be always heavy
in the heart of hearts
where treasures and secrets are kept?
Knowing the risks yet clinging
to selected characters and scenes,
just how far can anyone go
without being stopped by the very
enormity of it all, and then
realizing the need to break the bonds
to discover liberation
here and now.

Mellow

Tell me why you love me
and it will tell me more
about you than it will about me.
Explain what keeps you here
in these serene mountains
whose undulating ridges
envelope our lives.
Softly sheltering our days,
they form a gentler landscape
than the one you used to know.
I offer a tamer life
than the one you led before.
But you have chosen this
quieter, mellower way.
Still the fire of adventure
burns inside you.
I feel its warmth.

Change

Does aspiration fade with time
or simply settle into the fabric
of the consciousness
so integrally that
it doesn't stand out
as distinctly as it did
in the beginning of the quest
for Truth, Light, Oneness?
Or is it that ardor dims,
the fire burns less
intensely now,
glowing not raging,
sustaining warmth, giving energy,
not burning up in a conflagration
of *bhakti* and yearning?
As long as it burns
it gives precious Light.

Trust

Trying to move forward
while holding onto the past
is a trick rarely achieved,
requiring great power to move
all the bags and boxes
it's stuffed into.

But it's either forward
or back, no standing still,
so a choice is required.
There's really very little
option with the past already
gone, evaporated into
wisps of memories.

Yet the future is unfathomable
being unformed, unknown.
Faith enough to take a plunge
can make a good beginning,
trusting in life and in
something larger
than oneself.

Come Here

I didn't come here to be all morose and withdrawn.
I didn't come here to act all depressed and gloomy.
I came here to do something meaningful,
important for my progress, for evolving
into something higher, better
than what I have been before
in other less fortunate lives,
ones where I didn't know what I know now,
where things went even more amiss than they are going,
where the various problems and sufferings
may have seemed to me more pointless
than I can now understand them to be.
So I lament the depression, the needless sense
of separation from the inner *ananda*
which I believe to be innate,
the actual heart of existence,
the origin and core of what we are.
Why am I so lost and far away from it
when I know it is there inside me?
I have felt it before, experienced
the bliss within the heart of hearts.
But not today or yesterday have I found it.
It seems so far, like a dream of possibility,
shrouded in a mist of misery, smallness

and even anger, a surprise previously unknown,
or at least not acknowledged.
Some days it feels like there is only
one way to go and that is up.
So at least there is that.

At Your Feet

Bring me that vision again
of lying at your feet
like a small child asleep,
gathered up peacefully,
fully trusting in You.

Bring me that vision again
of your lotus feet above me
as I go about my day
aware of your presence
constantly with me.

Such is the nature of Grace
that worthiness is not an issue;
for if it were, this blessing
would never come to me.

Gifts

A touch of earth
to ground you in
the strength of
your mother

A touch of sky
to invite you
to rise up to
the heavens

A taste of sea
to energize you
for the tasks of
your journey

All these are
my blessings
to you.

The Valley

Tell me, please, about a new day,
a new place and way of being.
Speak to me of griefless skies,
of happy, hopeful contemplation.

I have heard that
there is a valley over the mountain
where people have discovered
renewal and even
transformation.

I am seeking to go there now,
finding my way up the hillside,
occasionally stumbling on rocks
while anticipating the view.

Weary

May I sink safely
into that soft dark space
which opens before me
so familiarly now.
Even with its sadness
it feels gentle and kind
in its enveloping welcome.
May it hold me sweetly
and also let me go
when courage has returned
to face another day.

Wanting

Yearning for meaning,
longing for acceptance,
yet tired of ego and
seeking rest from false
ambition.

Seeking a break from
wanting
anything from anyone.

Desirelessness offers
a great calm, a true freedom;
so if you want anything,
perhaps paradoxically,
you may want that.

Burning

Seared into the mind
the harsh thoughts forge
their own scorched earth
policy against hope
and creativity.
Their habitual nature
precludes opening to
new ideas and possibilities.
Can not and *will not*
burn away *can, will, might*
and leave behind ashes.
But resistance is not
futile and pessimism
and obstruction can be
defeated by inspiration,
fortitude and faith.
Otherwise why are we
here?

Dreaming

Bring me daffodils in winter
and holly berries in summer
as proof of the impossibility
of order in this universe.
Tell me tales of longing
where all wishes are granted,
all love requited and no one dies.
I want to live a life of miracles,
magic and wonder where
anything we dream of comes true
and nightmares never happen.
I want to hold your hand in mine,
look out upon the day and see
everyone everywhere in love
with each other.

Together

Constancy, fragility, hopefulness
intertwine throughout our days of living
together and serving in the project
we call our loving and fond partnership,
as we influence and mould each other.
The interactions evolve as we do,
changing in tone, varying in purpose,
rising in their aim and significance.
Wondering where I end and you begin,
I see you as so much a part of me
that differences are rarely perceived,
faintly sensed
like a waft of air.

Some Day

Some day we will see each other for the last time
not knowing that it will be the last,
that there will be no more time
for summing up appreciation,
for letting go of regret
or recriminations.
Some day there will be an end
to what we have here and now,
though no real end at all.
So let me tell you now
of my love and gratitude
and let that stand
as a final statement
when finality arrives.

The Cloud

Skimming along through decades
of photos in cloud storage
seems to trivialize personal history
or at least its real length and import.
Lightly passing a finger across a screen
can take you past births, graduations,
marriages, exotic travels,
or even deaths in a matter of seconds.
Having it speed by so quickly one can
wonder briefly and then dismiss
into the past what once was
marvelous and treasured. Oh well,
at least it's all there somewhere
and can be tapped into for reminiscences
if one can find it in all the
plenitude.

Fairly Benign

It's orchid-tending day
and as I go back and forth
from plant array to sink
I catch a faint and fleeting glimpse
of myself in a mirror,
a fairly benign looking
aging lady with wisps of hair
drifting over one eye.
So what about it? I ask.
Is this it, tending orchids,
writing mundane poetry,
waiting for something not yet known,
something enlightening, adding
meaning to the daily round?
This unnamed something must be there
waiting to emerge into fullness
like the next bud on the stem
of the quiescent small plant
in my window.
May it come.

After Another One

If there is one mass shooting every single day
how long will it take to wipe out the whole country?
Not being a mathematician and recognizing that
mass murderers seem to have varying ambitions
and styles of slaughter, it is hard to say.
So what are the chances for any of us that
going to the grocery store or a concert may
turn out to be a life-threatening event?
Of course we all know that life is uncertain,
that awful things happen, that people suffer,
that people die and not all of them in their own beds.
But this daily madness in what is supposed
to be a rational society is unbearable.
If we can't change this, what can we change?
I can't accept that we are a such an uncaring
and ineffectual country.
But maybe we are.

Take It

So what does it mean
to bandy about famous names
and snippets of their
not quite so famous ideas?
Does it do more than
indicate some form of erudition
or merely lead to a muddle
of confused thought and
mixed up directions for
the onward journey and what
to do when coming to
the proverbial and frequently
encountered fork in the road?
At least the ideas are present
in the swirling atmosphere
around the furrowed brows
of all the seekers as they
stand in the roadway and
contemplate the outstretched
options and yield to the
wisdom of Yogi Berra.

Passage

Dark eyes bordered by darker lashes
as abundant as the petals
on a sunflower
gaze from your young face
in a photo tucked away
languishing in a drawer
for eight years or more
and now brought to light
as a revealing contrast
and also for celebration.
Time takes a toll and losses
extract their heavy price
from energy and beauty.
You and she were together then,
captured happily by the lens
of a long-abandoned camera.
Together you lightly laughed
in a moment now vanished.
Though the memory remains
the jest has been forgotten.

My Kingdom

The kingdom of Anhedonia
lies on a vast flat plain
with little vegetation
to add interest or variety.
Its capital resembles
an ancient Medieval city
surrounded by thick stone walls.
Their height casts shadows,
darkening the streets and houses.
Within these bounds there is no laughter,
no music or fond caresses.
Within these bounds there is no flavor
to the food or to the life.
Every dish tastes like broccoli.
All the red wines taste like the white,
and no one has heard of chocolate.
Having long been the monarch,
change seems to be beyond my power,
for if it were not
it would have come by now.

III

Hope

Tell me truly that you know
the sun will rise tomorrow
and that the world will not end
in a hot toxic fog of man's creation,
brought on by incessant craving
for an endless flow of synthetic junk
and an incessant craving to feed
our desires to the full, for comfort and ease.
Tell me truly that we have the will
and the wisdom to stop fouling our own nest,
to rediscover respect for our mother
and give her reverence once again.

Planning an Exit

Expansion or contraction,
which way should it go—
downsizing to enable
an efficient exit even
though it means letting go
of so much with meaning
or upsizing to bring to
fruition all the potential
before the grand finale
even though it means leaving
more complications for those
ultimately left behind.
The tentative choice seems to
depend on the mood of
the day since I really want it
both ways.

Right Direction

Spare me the whys and wherefores.
Just give me the straight story
of what's going on and what needs
to be done from here on out.
I want to know my role and to
play it properly, heading in the
right direction—that is fully
forward, trying to build the future
and not wallow in the past.
So please give me the script,
a map and a compass,
and let me go.

Poor Poet

Pallid pedestrian poetry pales
beside the likes of Percy, William, *et al.*
The earth-bound poet plods on
pensively pondering possibilities
for getting a lift into higher spheres,
just a bit of inspiration
to carry her upward on a gust
of rising breeze towards
a creative sunrise.
She scouts her surroundings for
some inspiring stuff for solid content,
trying to make hay while the sun shines,
yet reaching out to find only
handfuls of sodden straw.

Quiet

I will be quiet today
since I have nothing to say.
No petty complaints,
no wisdom of saints
can emerge from me
as I drink my tea.
I will sit and reflect
with myself all bedecked
in colorful hues
from my hair to my shoes,
a perfect picture of calm
offering no words as balm.
While inner turmoil may reign
total peacefulness I feign,
for I need to be quiet today.

Small Things, Again

Let us find contentment
in small things—
softly green lambs' ears
glistening with the remnant
of last night's rain,
your coming home smiling,
dog's paws padding across
a gleaming wooden floor.
Let us take pleasure
in the daily goodness
that opens out before us,
in the simplicity
of the passing days,
treasuring them while we can.
Let me hold your hand
and look into your eyes
and feel the love between us.

Moonlit Walk

How sweet to be walking in the evening
by the light of a bright three-quarter moon,
swishing feet among dry brown leaves,
someone humming in the distance,
holding the leash of a small orange dog
which keeps chasing fleeting grasshoppers,
darting suddenly away from me
and toward them in the deep shrubbery.
This could go on all night
and every night and I would
be happy to keep repeating
the simple beauty of this time
and rediscovering
the peace in my heart.

Walking

Brilliant October, walking the trail
thinking about lima beans, collard greens and trout,
powerful fuel for the day.
His eyes well up, tears gleaming in their blueness.
Are you happy? Yes, grateful to be here,
to be able to do this.

Years ago at this brightly poignant season,
another hike in the blazing autumn sun,
wrapped with impending loss and present pain.
My eyes welled up, tears gleaming in their blueness.
Are you sad? Yes, that he cannot do this,
the child who could not walk anywhere
on that brilliant day.

Now ridge after ridge moves into the distance
forming a gently unfolding eternity,
an undulating vastness of varied hues.
A timeless somewhere of possibility
wells up before our eyes,
invoking infinity.

After Midnight

The late night quiet is my time.
It has been so ever since I was born,
coming into the world at midnight.
I am the guardian of that time
watching over the household,
making sure all is settled,
that no wayward beasts roam the halls,
before, being assured of safety,
giving myself permission
to sleep.

Small sounds come forth in the night,
creaking, crickets, engines of distant cars,
a branch breaking in the breeze
falling to earth with a soft thump.
None of these are the same when
they happen in the daytime.
It's the depth of the night that
gives them resonance, significance
as signals that it is time
for withdrawing into oneself
to rest.

Belonging

You have to belong to something
until you realize that
you belong to everything.
All of it is yours and
you belong everywhere—
the sea, the sky, the mountains,
all the continents and peoples
are in you and you in them.
There is no separation
at the very heart of things.
While there is variety
and differentiation,
all is in each, each in all
and all Divine.

Continuing

Tell me that the sun will shine tomorrow
and that I will hold your hand again.
Let me believe that there will be many
days of exploration and joy
in this bright and treasured place
where the progression of our days unfolds
with the simplicity and quiet ease
of a blossom opening in springtime.
I would like to live this way forever,
with you and me awakening again
and again to the same sense of promise.
Please help me maintain the illusion.

Foggy Day

Fog on Gilliam's Mountain
embraces the azaleas,
moves along the ridge
and settles softly
on the rhododendrons.

Oak and beech
stand out like spires
bursting through
the drifting misty veil
that cloaks the crest.

No sound penetrates
the simple quiet
of this rainy, chill
autumn afternoon,
sacred in its stillness.

American Chestnut

Climbing to the crest of the hillside
in the mist of the mountain morning,
the small band of treehuggers
reaches its goal, a lone chestnut tree.
It stands bedraggled in a clearing
opened out in its honor,
this dear survivor of the blight.
Standing in awe they note carefully
the shape and texture of its buds and leaves,
observe its battle wounds and scars,
admire its history and fortitude,
then quietly, solemnly proceed
down the slope with the haunting sense
of having travelled backwards in time.

Blue Ridge

A temple of trees lines the way
over the mountains as the road
winds toward the layered ridges
stretching out with an air
of offering infinity.
Counting them seems an impossibility
even though there must be
a certain number of them.
Confounded by their undulations
I simply bow down
before their beauty.

Perfect

Grounded in the earth,
aspiring toward heaven,
embodying the depth
and height of beauty,
the tree stands nobly
in fully expressive,
fine and purposeful detail.
What more can one hope for
in seeking perfection?

Morning Light

Whitening day leads to
sun's soft brilliance
shining, yet dimmed
by thick mountain mist,
hanging heavily
in the deepening folds
overshadowed by
the grand blue ridges
and high summits
far above them.
In time the light
will burn more brightly
seeming to dispel
the dense moisture
hovering there.
But really the mist
rises, rises,
rises again,
offering itself
as sweet sacrifice
to the sun.

Heart of the Woods

Is the woodpecker in love
with the sound of his pecking,
or perhaps he is
with the tree he is wrecking.
Is his rat-a-tat-tat
a delight to his ears,
does his thock-thock-thock
reduce him to tears
of joy as he beats
his resonating rhythm
through the woods
as he eats
one more bug.

Loving It

small dogs in the sunshine
russet fur against green grass
rolling twisting back-rubbing joy
tiny white teeth exposed in a laugh
violets as a carpet under racing paws
wood pansies like a bread crumb trail
leading us home in the warmth
tumultuous treetops swaying in the breeze
pileated woodpecker flitting and hammering
in the hollowness of catalpa and beech
hearts surging for the love of it all

Rainy Walk

Two small wet dogs in the rain
dart and scamper their way
to shelter under the big oak
in its island of grass and leaves,
concluding their customary walk
before turning back to home.
They are content with their small world
spanning the distance between house
and gigantic ancient oak tree.
This is enough for them.
I wish it was for me.

Wet Carpet

The furry damp dog
pads along the fallen leaves
forming a soggy carpet
under the massive oak,
no longer providing shelter
from the autumnal downpour.
Unheeding he makes his way,
savoring each tiny puddle
cupped in each curling leaf.
Happily he examines
each branch and twig
awaiting his inspection,
until he choses one
to bring indoors as his prize
for being such a good dog
with a keen eye for sticks.

Chill

Coming into winter
with low expectations
for the passing of the days,
I wonder if they would
turn out better if
I hoped for more.
But there's no changing it
now that it's underway,
for we get only one beginning
to each and every season
and what's gone is surely gone.
So best make a better start
next time around.

Snowbound

Relishing the quiet, remote, isolated
sense of being cut off
from all the usual busyness,
the daily pulsing pressure
of this and that required
by the demanding others,
being snowbound feels beautiful,
luxurious and sweet.
The icicles out the window
gleam with diamond brightness
as the sun rises and reveals
them longer day by day,
reassuring me of my
freedom.

Seasons

The earth underfoot feels hard as stone
in the frozen early morning.
The ice in the birdbath has expanded
upwards forming a shiny flat cap
perched uninvitingly and daring
any birds to land upon it.
Another winter has come at last,
soon to be followed by another spring.
After many decades you know it,
feeling the rapid cycling of the seasons
almost as moving from one month to the next.
It all seems very dependable
though rather hurried and you want
it all to slow down and pace itself,
much as you want to do in your own
comings and goings as time surges on.
You want to savor what you have,
experiencing its fullness, exploring
its length and breadth, tasting its flavors
and really living it while you can.
So delight in the frozen earth and
let spring take its time to come.

Blizzard Walk

The dutiful little snow-encrusted dog
pushed steadily through the increasing depths
following his accustomed path along with
his determined lady who insisted that he
accomplish his nightly emptying even in a
blizzard.

It was all her fault, not his, that they
came home caked with ice and the sense of
having gone on a fruitless mission at almost
midnight.

Doggie loyalty seems a lot more admirable
than human
folly.

Wet Dog

Rainfall gathers on the leaves
in my garden,
pooling in tiny lakes
among the stones
along the sodden pathway.
Even the squirrels
are taking shelter up high
in their lofty nests.
They know better how to hide
than I do now,
getting soaked while bringing home
a very wet dog
who loves every puddle,
laughs at the rain,
eagerly seeks the comfort
of a good toweling off.
I wish someone would do that
for me.

My Forest

A ray of golden light proceeds
through the dense high foliage
to brighten the forest floor below,
penetrating the shady depths
with patches of surprising brilliance.
The deep woods hold many secrets,
but even these are vulnerable
to revelation when touched by beams
of surpassing brightness and beauty;
for the coming dawn
cannot be denied
and truth will be known.

IV

Hug

I lean over to reach her frail
ninety-six-year-old shoulders
saying I'll give her a hug before I go,
nearly tumbling as I extend myself over the recliner
where she sits deeply ensconced and smiling faintly.
I reach the bony shoulders and regain my balance.
With her hands in her lap she looks up at me
and says, "I guess I could have given you a hug."
So is it all taking now and no more giving?
After so many years of mothering
is she spent, through with it all?
Is she content to be the queen bee and have me
be a tireless acolyte; I hesitate to say *drone*?
This is probably the way it is.
It's certainly the way it feels.

Chocolate Wafers

A cheerful cousin came to visit
my dear ancient mother today.
Struggling with her aphasia and
striving to maintain joviality
he nearly took all her special
cookies, instead of just a few.
Ever seeking to be gracious,
he finally did conclude that they
were offered just to him and not
to his daughter's basketball team.
So dear ancient mother still has
her little stack of scrumptious wafers
and her favorite and only nephew
enjoyed a pleasantly confused teatime
with his dear favorite and only aunt.

Another Easter

Chilly Easter morning
without children or chocolate in celebration,
just very grown-up nieces and
a very ancient mom slowly
consuming an assisted-living brunch
of turkey, gravy, rice, asparagus
and nutless carrot cake topped
with vanilla ice cream gradually
melting into a lake on an equally
pale plate placed close by
in order to lessen drips and spills
onto ancient mom's traditional
bright-flowered Sunday jacket.
Remembering all the lovely
Easter baskets ancient mom had
prepared for her chicks through decades,
I need to smile and feel
grateful.

Hairdresser

Pamela scrubs and rubs the frothy foam
in the pure whiteness of my mother's hair,
so white that even wet it doesn't darken.
My mother squints, peering at me across the room,
glasses off, hearing aid out, beginning to notice
that I am there, just arrived, observing.
Her face seems diminished without
the poofy cloud of softness,
looking much like a blanched walnut shell,
all wrinkled, lined and rather small.
Pamela brings out a fluffy towel, then a brush,
curling segments of hair, brushing, drying,
the heat expanding across the room.
She works magic and transforms the tiny, pale head
into an elegant and charming form.
Glasses back in place, hearing aid applied,
my mother beams at me across the room.
Order is restored.

Oxygen

Her voice rises slightly,
faintly heard above the pulse
of the squat concentrator
as it pushes oxygen
along a transparent tube
which extends across the floor
to the large blue recliner
where my mother sits ensconced.
"Have you met Jenny?
Jenny, this is my daughter."
A gracious introduction
offered again and again
to the same cast members
in this long-running play
where my mother plays herself
as a ninety-six-year-old
and I play the role of
an obedient daughter.

Another Christmas

"I'm ninety-six years old and may not
be here next year," my mother said
after learning that her youngest child
would be driving around the streets of
another city to see Christmas lights
with friends instead of being with her.
"Yes, that's possible," I replied, "but
I surely hope you will be,"
trying to put a good face on things
and not add to the distress.
After all, it wasn't me who made
this choice and I also didn't want
to guilt-trip my baby sister,
who had devotedly attended
more Christmases than I could count.
So there I sat holding the tension
and perplexity while mentally
grasping at straws for some good news
to share and to try to cheer up
my precious dear old mom,
while also reminding myself that
there are some things you just
can't control and hoping that
she will be here next year.

Puttin' on the Ritz

Mr. Goldbloom wears a top hat
as elegantly as anyone,
graciously introducing the acts.
White-haired ladies sing
as earnestly as anyone,
though with excess tremolo.
Cheerful nurses dance
as vigorously as anyone,
though completely out of step.
It's the first annual variety show
at the Lodge in the Blue Ridge.
So when a disgruntled guest
grumbles, rudely asserting
"I could sing better than that,"
the offense goes largely unnoticed
amidst general good humor,
the simple joy of being
alive and ready to sing.

Ray

Gray-haired, glint-eyed singer,
woo the ladies in the front row
with your ageless charm.
Sing to them the jazz beats,
the show tunes of their glory days
and redden their cheeks with excitement.
It's a wonder how the dynamic
of male-female attraction throbs
on so tirelessly, enlivening the atmosphere,
making it crackle with heightened energy,
bringing warmth and longing into play.
So do us all a favor
and sing on.

Holiday Photo

We stand somewhat uneasily
posing for a photograph
documenting a rare event—
our parents' four children
all together in one place.
Adjusting position studiedly
behind our mother's wheelchair
some of us gently place
a hand upon her shoulder.
Mother lifts her chin up
giving her a haughty air.
While three of us face forward
smiling for the camera,
one scowls faintly, turns slightly,
expressing the ambivalence
that lies behind it all.

Born Sad

"I was born sad," she murmured,
my ancient mother,
from the depths of her recliner.
Seeing her looking fatigued, pale
and expressionless,
I had asked if she felt sad.
Getting this disturbing response,
trying to offer comfort,
her next comments are unintelligible.
Mildly panicking, seeking to grasp
the words spoken with precious effort,
I finally make out some phrases:
"The tunic with three-quarter sleeves—
that's the one I want."
Sometimes one can only try.

Meltdown

Meltdown over petty geriatric requests—
septuagenarian daughter dutifully delivers shopping
to ancient mother who then squeezes red juice box
all over herself, wheelchair, table, carpet and
then mutters inaudibly expecting responses
from daughter who is rushing to and fro
to clean up ancient mother and the mess
and as if that wasn't enough ancient mother next
directs rapidly aging daughter to re-transcribe
all the birthdays, anniversaries, appointments
from the calendar which daughter brought
and transcribed all of these onto a few days ago,
since ancient mother now prefers the
calendar doting precious granddaughter
brought in a swoop-in visit yesterday.
So dutiful daughter tediously transcribes
all the aforesaid events onto the pages
while ancient mother mutters,
"I'm so sorry to make you do this,"
to which daughter has no speakable reply.
This being accomplished, ancient mother
requests the reading of emails and
daughter moves to bring wheelchair closer to
computer and computer table closer

to wheelchair, upon which later action
computer decides to collapse from
its stand onto the floor with a jumble of
cords, a baby monitor and the CD player
with the unused audio book which dutiful
septuagenarian daughter brought at her
mother's request two days before. While dutiful
daughter is bending over the chaotic mess
on the floor seeking to put things right,
ancient mother speaks her only response
to this, "Give me my water," she says.
Dutiful daughter does this and then
proceeds to bring order to chaos,
turn on the computer and read
messages from siblings one of whom
is preparing to go to Virgin Gorda
for an entire month. Ancient mother
seems surprised and asks for tissues
to put up her sleeve for the trip
downstairs to hear Jack and Polly Crabtree
play bluegrass in the dining room.
Tissues supplied, off we go.
Jack and Polly are in good form
and announce: "Jack is going to sing
in Nepali in honor of the Chinese New Year."
Whatever next….

Sunnyside

Her hand felt cool, almost cold
as she reached out to hold mine,
her thin wooly-clad arm extending
out from the depth of her chair.
She had not ever done this,
reaching out to hold my hand,
since I was a little girl and
needed her protection crossing a street.
Now my mother needs my protection,
concern, and even my voice to speak up
for her, to tell others what she cannot.
Now sitting close together
in the big hall of the Lodge
we let song pour over us,
bluegrass, gospel, and the blues.
The Sunnyside Band is here,
pickin' and singin' away
like there's no tomorrow.
And maybe there isn't.

Sweet Mama, Transplanted

She had left behind
her view of Peak's Knob,
the mountain crest which
she had seen from her window
since she was a young mother
tending me and then
three more well-loved babes.
She had left behind
her own blue boudoir,
blue parlor, and even
the treasured blue hydrangeas,
long since drying up in
her now-abandoned garden.
Courageously transplanted
to another, far distant town
with a view of another
less distant mountain,
she took solace in the Blue Ridge
and discovered a late-life
love of bluegrass.

Assisted Living Elevator Talk

"Your family is lucky to have you,"
he said to me from the back of
an elevator full of furniture.
"I'm helping someone who doesn't
have anyone like you," he explained.
"For whatever reasons of
family history and relationships,
some people don't have anyone
like you who cares and looks after them.
It takes compassion," he continued.
"Some people just don't really know
what compassion truly means.
It's not just a feeling,
you have to practice it."
"Yes," I agreed, gesturing to my chest.
"It needs to be heartfclt."
We nodded to each other
as the door closed.

Son

I tried to teach him to say "spectacles"
in the belief that the word "glasses" could lead to
confusion.

I tried to teach him the alphabet
by making him a brightly colored poster for his
bedroom wall.

I tried to help him find enlightenment
by taking him to an ashram on the other side
of the world.

And then he grew up to teach me
more than I could ever have learned
without him.

Tides Inn

Remembering Carter's Creek years ago,
a peacefulness there, a sailboat drifting,
as I clutched a small bronze figure of a bird
and hoped for the future, for little children
of my own, imagining tiny boys
with dark or golden hair, wearing Eton suits,
their lovely small limbs rosy with youth
racing across lawns in quest of butterflies.
Those were dreams to push one forward into life,
visions to build upon, to sustain you.
These images linger even now
and have power beyond present truth,
for they were driven by hope, created by love.

Openness

Walking across a former field,
now a parking lot,
noting the vast azure above
observable by the absence of trees,
I recall the massive midwestern sky—
standing beneath it with my eldest son
out in Richmond, Indiana,
and then later with my youngest
in the wideness of central Ohio.
What times of possibility they were,
all openness and pervaded
with the sense that great and good things
could happen out there in that spaciousness.
Time and landscapes are narrowing
the options, enforcing constraints
even as we seek to expand.

Closeted

The closets are filled with memorabilia.
At least that's what I call it,
the boxes of clothing, letters and files,
the mementoes of lost children,
proof that they once were really here,
warm and fully dimensional
in this house, sleeping and waking,
sharing stories, observations
from their singular points of view.
Having lost them, how can I
also lose the rocking horse,
the bowling shirt, the tall black boots?
Having lost them, now can I
leave this place and all the cues
which so vividly prompt visions—
painful, comforting and sweet,
clasped closely and examined
each as its own true treasure
in the quiet vault of the heart.

Warm Springs

To take you there,
to give you the warmth,
the comfort, the ease
of these gentle waters,
for you to drift,
peaceful in the softness,
the flow of the springs,
the light-glinted pool
as if it were made
just for you, to soothe,
to bless and heal you
as I longed for it to do.

All this and more, hoped,
imagined, yet not
to come to pass
in this lifetime.
The stream flows on,
filling, refreshing
others, as the flow
of time leaves behind
our days together.

Will these come again,
fragments of life shared,
joining in some future
not yet dreamed or known?
If so, I would welcome
a way to make this
all that it could be
for you of the joy
of warm springs and light.

Blue Tattoos

The tattoos were still fresh
on his ankles, intricate starbursts
of blue and rose.
Their form accented his grace
as he stepped into the green ocean
at Cherry Grove.
He had gotten them expansively
foreseeing days of richness,
a future free of suffering.
Their color and style
belied the deep fear of ending
expressed only once.
He had risen gently with a wave,
speaking as the swell lifted us up,
of the possibility of dying,
a catch in his voice.
Love and reassurance given,
settling into the sand's softness,
he rested.

Mourning

Monticello Mountain in the morning,
sunlight sifting through the leaves
as the early autumn day breaks
revealing anticipation and sorrow.
What flowers do we bring now
to these graves so long honored
season after season placing there
flowers for each time, bright and fine—
roses, which the deer consume,
carnations and chrysanthemums,
which they browse past and ignore,
also daffodils, but now a wreath
for the depth of grief in winter.
Long ago when first we knew this place,
I dug through the snow to frozen flowers,
ice-encrusted gems of crimson and white,
struggling to release them as if to release life.
I cried out to my lost son,
"What are you doing here?"
Now many years on I finally know
that the question was misplaced.
He is not there.

Grape Soda Clock

It hung on his wall as an amusing retro touch
in his eclectically crowded apartment
now seeming so empty without him.
Its glow illuminated the room beaming
out its message in support of grape soda.

Comforting in its ordinariness,
it became her nightly companion
as she lay on his green sofa
waiting for sleep to overtake grief,
helped along by a glass of single malt.

Days passed, books were packed,
tables, chairs, rugs disappeared.
An old friend admired the clock
and it too joined the desertion,
leaving her to sleep in darkness.

Honoring

I want to know that there is time enough
for remembrance, for honoring
the lost ones, the missing persons
who featured so powerfully
in my life but now are gone.
I want to know that I can create
volumes and monuments and tributes
to them almost without end,
so that others in the far future
will know their names, their stories,
their worthiness of love and honoring,
even though others will not see
the beauty of their forms,
even though others will not hear
the sound of their laughter
or their fine eloquence.
I want to know that there can be a kind
of immortality in remembrance.

Lightly

The lady has grieved too long,
unfairly clinging to those
she lovingly cherishes.
The power of attachment
needs to loosen its grasp,
liberating everyone—
those who have gone and those left behind.
Long may she love—fully, but lightly.
May her love spread out gently,
always like the dandelion
seeds wafting on wispy wings,
traveling far and wide on the breeze.
May her love settle softly
upon them
as a blessing.

Young Man

Young man, if you see a white-haired lady
looking at you with soft, even affectionate,
expression, you may assume that she is
wistfully wishing that she was young again
and able to catch your interest.
Do not be saddened to know
that instead she is looking at you
because she is remembering a lost son
who once was your age or once
wore his hair as you do.
Perhaps his complexion resembled yours
or he once wore a similar shirt
or stood as you do, leaning against the wall.
Do not be saddened to know the cause,
but rather be pleased that you can give her
the pleasure of remembrance.

Singing

The lady remembered well the past—
she sang of days full of joy and hope,
of holding her young children in her arms.
She sang of sunny summer days sitting
on the grass with glasses of white wine
under towering tulip trees, believing
that all was good and would forever be,
that safety and security were given
and abundance would forever flow through the years
as everyone grew and progressed into
self-actualized and grown up beings.
The lady remembers still the losses—
she sings of the overclouding of the sun,
the dimming of the light, the wave surges
of grief breaking on the shore of her very self and
nearly drowning as they carried her out to sea.
She sings too of her salvation, being rescued
by brave, beautiful beings with pure hearts
who helped her find her way home, comforting her
with their songs of love and faith until
she found her own voice again.

Epilogue

Waking Up

I woke up after having a dream about a woman who had thought that two of her sons had died but then she realized that it was a dream and she was so relieved to know that all was as she had wanted it to be that everyone she loved was really there really alive and that things could go on as she had expected them to so I wondered if my sense of reality was faulty too and if all that I thought had happened to me was really only a dream and that there had been no tragedies and that I would wake up and find everyone I loved was somewhere or other where I could see them or know about them and know that they were all right and doing what they wanted or at least what was best for them and that God was in His/Her Heaven and all was really right with the world so wouldn't it be great if all the miseries that I thought had happened were only part of a long complex dream that only the good things had happened that is only the things I thought I wanted to happen really did happen but then I knew that couldn't be true since one can't be selective in such matters and either it is all true and real or none of it is so if it all is real then there is so much nightmare that I want it to be unreal and a dream but if I can choose then what would I choose I thought I would choose being a young girl with soft blond hair in the sunshine on a summer morning being in love for the first time with a boy with black Irish good looks walking in shady groves of oak trees finding a soul mate later than I expected being a young mother with a sweet little dark-haired baby in my arms and then two more lovely little ones and seeing them all grow up into great big glowing beings who stride about the earth on fine strong legs and laugh and delight in being loved and loving and writing stories and throwing pots and designing engines in a world that receives them with open arms that is surely what I would choose I would want to forget about violence dark nights inner torments betrayals disillusionment cynical people who have no faith in human nature or the future of the planet who think in terms of you and me of us and them and not of all of us as one so if I forgot about them maybe everything would be all one at least for me but that would not be enough because it should be so for everyone and just for some of us is not enough because everyone else matters too I would remember the old lady who said don't ever get both old and fat and I would keep trying not to though I want to live long but not get old or fat who doesn't have those kinds of hopes though usually without expecting to realize them but how real and true are these remembrances and avoidances are they only the outer crust of what makes up a person this particular one at least though I think everyone has an array of these circling through and around their heads thought emotion that is not the sum total of who they are since there is something more something truer better more real very deep inside which is truly true really real immortal eternal pure divine which will gradually come forth express itself in ever-growing lightness making the swirling anxieties memories hopes stop vibrating in their friction-driven way harmonizing all the thoughts feelings speculations into a wholeness settling the conflicts once and for all and making me and you and everyone one day just what we should be really want to be and that is to be ourselves.